Cambridge
Travel Guide

Quick Trips Series

No part of this publication may be reproduced, stored in a retrieval system, or transmitted, in any form or by any means without the prior written permission of the publisher, nor be otherwise circulated in any form of binding or cover other than that in which it is published and without similar condition being imposed on the subsequent purchaser. If there are any errors or omissions in copyright acknowledgements the publisher will be pleased to insert the appropriate acknowledgement in any subsequent printing of this publication. Although we have taken all reasonable care in researching this book we make no warranty about the accuracy or completeness of its content and disclaim all liability arising from its use.

Copyright © 2016, Astute Press
All Rights Reserved.

Table of Contents

CAMBRIDGE — 6
- Customs & Culture 11
- Geography 13
- Weather & Best Time to Visit 16

SIGHTS & ACTIVITIES: WHAT TO SEE & DO — 19
- King's College Grounds & Chapel 19
- Fitzwilliam Museum 21
- Cambridge University Botanic Gardens 22
- The Backs 24
- Punting on the River Cam 25
- Kettle's Yard 26
- Scott Polar Research Institute 27
- Sedgwick Museum of Earth Sciences 29
- Shepreth Wildlife Park 31
- Duxford Imperial War Museum 33
- Newmarket Races 35

BUDGET TIPS — 39
- Accommodation 39

   Home From Home Guest House...39
   Alpha Milton Guest House 40
   Cambridge Colleges..41
   Chapel Street B&B 42
   Arbury Lodge..43

🌐 Restaurants, Cafés & Bars 44
   Sticky Beaks Café...44
   Camyoga Café 45
   The Table 46
   Clowns Café..47
   Gardenia..49

🌐 Shopping 50
   Grafton Centre 50
   Cambridge Markets 51
   Mill Road Shopping Mile 53
   Jacks on Trinity..54
   Cambridge Toy Shop..55

🌐 Entry Requirements 57
   Health Insurance 59
   Travelling with pets 60

🌐 Airports, Airlines & Hubs...62
   Airports...62
   Airlines 65
   Hubs 67
   Sea Ports 67
   Eurochannel 69

🌐 Money Matters 69
   Currency 69
   Banking/ATMs 70
   Credit Cards 70
   Tourist Tax..71
   Claiming back VAT..71
   Tipping Policy 72

🌐 Connectivity 73

Mobile Phones 73
Dialling Code 75
Emergency Numbers 75
🌐 GENERAL INFORMATION **76**
Public Holidays 76
Time Zone 77
Daylight Savings Time 77
School Holidays 77
Trading Hours 78
Driving Policy 79
Drinking Policy 80
Smoking Policy 80
Electricity 81
Food & Drink 81
Events 84
Websites of Interest 88
Travel Apps 88

CAMBRIDGE TRAVEL GUIDE

Cambridge

Cambridge in East Anglia is famously known as a leading university city and has a long history stretching back to the Bronze Age. The University of Cambridge was founded in 1209 and is among the top five universities in the world.

CAMBRIDGE TRAVEL GUIDE

Evidence of a 3,500 year old farmstead was found where Fitzwilliam College now stands. For those interested in ancient history, there has been a recent find of a major Anglo-Saxon burial site.

Over the centuries the city has suffered from fire and flood but in 1349 the Black Death wiped out many of the scholars, clergy and general population. Across the country a third of English clergy had perished in the grip of this dreadful disease and Gonville Hall, Trinity Hall, Corpus Christi and Clare Colleges were established soon after to train new clergymen.

Cambridge was granted city status in 1951 and this is quite unusual as it doesn't have a cathedral. It comes under the Diocese of Ely where the magnificent Ely cathedral is locally known as the Ship of the Fens.

CAMBRIDGE TRAVEL GUIDE

Peterhouse was the first college in 1284 and many others followed. The oldest university building is the School of Pythagoras in St. John's College; originally a town house it is still in active use today.

Construction of many of the colleges, in particular King's College and Chapel occurred through the reigns of Henry VI through to Henry VIII. From 1594 to 1800 the university and town were in something of decline and all building work stopped. By late Victorian times construction was again underway including Girton College, the first women's college.

Visitors from around the globe come to see the impressive university buildings and learn about the rich history the museums and collections offer. The University

CAMBRIDGE TRAVEL GUIDE

of Cambridge has a worldwide reputation for academic achievement and is one of the oldest universities in the world. World-class research is carried out at some of the Colleges and there are many unusual customs and terminology that can be traced back hundreds of years.

There are nine museums and collections which are open to the public throughout the year. All of the College Chapels and most of the Colleges are open to the public at certain times.

There are 29 Colleges for undergraduates, including three that are for women only and two that are for postgraduates only. Approximately 25,000 students are at the university at any one time, two thirds as undergraduates and the remainder on postgraduate courses.

CAMBRIDGE TRAVEL GUIDE

The most unusual course that is offered at the university is Anglo-Saxon, Norse and Celtic (ASNAC). Cambridge is the only university in the country to offer this. The most popular courses are generally medicine, languages, law and mathematics. Around 15,000 hopefuls apply for a place every year, but with only 3,300 places or so on offer at any one time there is always a lot of disappointment.

There has always been an element of rivalry between the "town" and "gown" members of Cambridge as in so many other university towns worldwide. The term was coined in the Middle Ages when the students wore long black gowns to protect them against studying in unheated buildings and draughty halls. The gown also had a social status, as it was impractical for manual work and set the students apart from the citizens in the town. Even today

CAMBRIDGE TRAVEL GUIDE

local communities will clash with universities over economic, political and demographic issues.

Walking tours from Wheeler Street Tourist Office are a great way to learn about this centre of great architectural interest and esteemed seat of learning and there are panoramic views from the top of Great St. Mary's Church. Most of the city attractions are based on or around the university, its history and museums. The city is famous as well for the annual Cambridge v Oxford Boat Race held on the River Thames.

The city centre is made up of mainly commercial buildings, with ancient and modern architecture rubbing shoulders, and many of these buildings belong to and are used by the University of Cambridge. Some areas of the centre are traffic free and with large green spaces such as

CAMBRIDGE TRAVEL GUIDE

Parker's Piece and Midsummer Common there are plenty of places to cycle or walk. The cobbled streets are full of book-laden students moving about between classes and grabbing a bite to eat or a quick coffee as they dash off to another lecture.

🌐 Customs & Culture

The Cambridge Corn Exchange was built in 1868 and was officially opened in 1875. Through the years it has been used for motor shows, boxing matches, wrestling and roller skating. Through the Second World War it was a centre for local women to clean rifles.

Today it is a popular venue for theatre and music groups as well as comedians and features on many touring performer's schedules. Famous names that have played

CAMBRIDGE TRAVEL GUIDE

there include David Bowie, Elkie Brooks, Lily Allen and the Manic Street Preachers.

The city is known for its technology and science parks so it is only fitting that every year there should be the Cambridge Science Festival. Every spring 200 or so events welcome 30,000 visitors to talks, displays, demonstrations and hands-on activities. For anyone considering a career in this field or just very interested in science this is a great opportunity to talk to the experts.

If you want to experience one of the best summer fairs plan your visit to Cambridge for the first Saturday in June. On Midsummer Common ten hours of arts and crafts, films, live music and theatre draw people together. The event is free and there are parades, pageants, battle re-enactments and tricks from the Cambridge Circus

CAMBRIDGE TRAVEL GUIDE

performers. There is plenty to see and do for children and adults and there are lots of local foods to try as well as locally brewed ales and wines.

For lovers of the Bard and the written word the Cambridge Shakespeare Festival runs through July and August in the picturesque settings of private gardens in the different universities. Wordfest in April and November is a chance for established and aspiring authors to showcase their talents in a series of events and shows.

The Cambridge Junction hosts clubs and events for young people as well as comedy, dance and theatre with cutting edge performances. For theatre goers the ADC Theatre is the oldest University playhouse in the country and along with the Corpus Playroom offers a yearly programme of professional and exciting performances.

CAMBRIDGE TRAVEL GUIDE

Cambridge Folk Festival is one of the most famous and long running festivals for this type of music in the world. The three or four day long weekend event is traditionally held at Cherry Hinton Hall a few miles from Cambridge. Tickets sell out fast for this festival which is around the end of July to the beginning of August every year. Different stages and arenas are set up to make the most of the performances and many famous names in folk music perform more than once over the weekend. There is a campsite, workshops, music and instrument stalls and of course lots of different foods and drinks to try.

🌎 Geography

Cambridge sits on the River Cam in the county of Cambridgeshire, East Anglia. The city is 50 miles north of London and in 2011 the population was 124,000, with

CAMBRIDGE TRAVEL GUIDE

25,000 being students. A large proportion of the workforce is in professional, managerial or admin jobs and the number of people with a degree or higher level education is above the national average.

The terrain is low-lying and only rises between 20ft and 80ft above sea level. Many of the surrounding wetlands have been drained over the years as the town has expanded. Cambridge was named in 2010 as one of the most beautiful cities in the world and tourism generates an income of over £350 million every year.

Cambridge is also known as the Silicon Fen due to the large number of technology and science industries that are at the heart of its economic structure. Innovation and education have made Cambridge one of the UK's fastest

CAMBRIDGE TRAVEL GUIDE

growing regions as well as ground-breaking medical advances at Addenbrookes Hospital.

Transport is excellent with rail links between the city centre and London Kings Cross as well as Norwich and Birmingham. From the main bus station in Drummer Street there are connections for local, national and international destinations.

Road access is good with the M11 and A14 roads being a few minutes away. The park and ride system is great and well worth considering if you arriving by car. Parking in Cambridge is difficult and can be very expensive and there is a confusing system of one-way streets to contend with as well.

CAMBRIDGE TRAVEL GUIDE

Cambridge has a small airport mainly for charter and private aircraft, although there are limited flights to Switzerland, Jersey and Italy. For a wider range of domestic and international flights London Stansted Airport is only half an hour away.

Cambridge is a city that is bicycle mad. Thousands of cyclist's everyday makes use of this cheap and efficient way to get around. The official autumn census shows a figure of 7,000 cyclists per day going in and out of the town and surrounding villages. There is a network of cycle paths for commercial and recreational use crossing the city and outskirts and bicycles can be hired from many shops by visitors. Routes 11 and 51 of the National Cycle Network pass through the city.

CAMBRIDGE TRAVEL GUIDE

🌐 Weather & Best Time to Visit

The weather in Cambridge is influenced by the Gulf Stream and officially classed as a maritime climate. Located in one of the driest areas of Great Britain the annual rainfall is half the national average and some years less than that. The sun shines for about 1,500 hours per year which is about average.

Spring in Cambridge is pleasant. The University Botanic Garden is coming into bloom and everywhere the trees in the parks and on the famous Cambridge Backs are beginning to unfurl their leaves. The night time low of 3°C quickly rises and in the daytime a comfortable 17°C can be reached. As the weather warms up lighter clothes and pretty colours make a change from winter coats and drab browns and greys.

CAMBRIDGE TRAVEL GUIDE

At the height of summer a daytime temperature of 23°C is achieved and locals and visitors alike can be found punting on the River Cam and having picnics in the many open spaces. Even in the evenings the low of 10°C is not too bad and you will only need a light wrap if you are out after dark. Cambridge regularly has the highest annual summer temperature across the country.

By the time the autumn months come round and the leaves begin to fall so does the mercury. Daytime can be warm and still reach 19°C but the mornings and evenings will definitely be feeling chillier. The days get shorter and through the night a low of 3°C can be felt. The central heating goes on and the shorts go away for another year, warm jumpers and a jacket are a must.

CAMBRIDGE TRAVEL GUIDE

Snow does fall in Cambridge but not very often. The winter low of 1°C means it is never really cold enough for snow and frost to stay around for very long. If it is windy it will of course feel much colder so it is probably wise to go out equipped with hat, gloves and a scarf. The high in winter is 10°C although it has been known to be considerably warmer.

CAMBRIDGE TRAVEL GUIDE

Sights & Activities: What to See & Do

🌏 King's College Grounds & Chapel

King's Parade

Cambridge

CB2 1ST

Tel: +44 1223 331212

www.kings.cam.ac.uk/

CAMBRIDGE TRAVEL GUIDE

Visitors are welcome to King's and can attend choral services in the Chapel and wander freely through the college grounds.

The Chapel was founded in 1441 by Henry VI but it wasn't properly completed until nearly one hundred years under the Tudor Dynasty. It is a fine example of Gothic architecture and the 26 stained glass windows and chancel screen are some of the finest ones of the time.

The peaceful gardens have a large central fountain with a statue dedicated to Henry VI in the centre with Religion and Philosophy sitting beneath him.

Tickets to King's College Grounds and Chapel cost £7.50 for adults and £5 for children, senior citizen and students.

CAMBRIDGE TRAVEL GUIDE

Opening times vary but are generally about 9.30am to 3pm Monday to Saturday and 1pm to 2.30pm on Sunday. There are often closures for private events and exams so it is worth calling ahead or checking on the website to avoid disappointment.

Fitzwilliam Museum

Trumpington Street

Cambridge

CB2 1RB

Tel: +44 1223 332900

www.fitzmuseum.cam.ac.uk/

Over 300,000 visitors go to the Fitzwilliam Museum every year. This is the art and antiquities museum for the University of Cambridge and was founded in 1816. A bequest from the 7th Viscount FitzWilliam of his art and

CAMBRIDGE TRAVEL GUIDE

book collection along with a donation of £100,000 to house it meant that future generations could share these exciting treasures.

The five main departments are Coins and Medals; Manuscripts and Printed Books; Paintings, Drawings and Prints; Applied Arts and Antiquities. There are collections within these departments from Greece and Rome, Sudan, Ancient Egypt, China, Japan and Korea as well as displays from Western Asia and art from Cyprus.

Virginal manuscript music from 16th century composers such as Thamas Tallis, Orlando Gibbons and William Byrd can be found as well as paintings by the great masters; Reuben, Titian, Van Dyck and Picasso.

Admission to this wonderful museum is free but any donations are greatly appreciated and help towards the upkeep of the museum. The opening times are Tuesday to Saturday 10am to 5pm and Sunday noon to 5pm.

🌐 Cambridge University Botanic Gardens

1 Brookside

Cambridge

CB2 1JE

Tel: +44 1223 336265

www.botanic.cam.ac.uk/

The 40 acres of the Cambridge University Botanic Garden is an oasis of calm and colour in the fast moving pace of city life. Unbelievably it is right in the city centre and is a

CAMBRIDGE TRAVEL GUIDE

wonderful escape for workers and students to take a break through their busy days.

Different displays make up the gardens and demonstrate ways of gardening with reduced watering as well as species from across the globe. In the Glasshouses 3,000 species represent Tropical Rainforests, Arid Lands, Oceanic Islands, South Africa and SW Australia and a section of Life Before Flowers.

The lake makes pretty setting for the glasshouses and across the gardens there are herbaceous borders, rock gardens, scented gardens and gardens for the different seasons. Events are held thought the year to inform and educate people about the importance of gardening.

CAMBRIDGE TRAVEL GUIDE

The gardens open daily at 10am and are open until 6pm in the summer months with earlier closing in the winter. There is a Café for refreshments and in the Botanic Garden Shop small gifts and gardening related items can be purchased. Adults pay £4.50 with concessions paying £4 and children under 16 get in free.

🌍 The Backs

Queens Road

Cambridge

This area gets its name as it is where the backs of many of the Cambridge colleges run down to meet the winding River Cam. The area runs from the bridge at Magdalen Street in the north to the bridge at Silver Street in the south.

CAMBRIDGE TRAVEL GUIDE

Historically used as an area for growing fruit or grazing livestock this picturesque strip of green is now a popular place for walkers and joggers, families and friends to while away a few hours.

It is an ideal opportunity for taking fantastic photos of many of the seven Colleges, some which are on both sides of the river.

On the west bank is Magdalene and on the east bank Trinity, Trinity Hall, Clare and King's can be found. St. John's has buildings on both sides spanned by the Bridge of Sighs as does Queens' spanned by the Mathematical Bridge.

CAMBRIDGE TRAVEL GUIDE

🌐 Punting on the River Cam

Scudamore's

Granta Place

Cambridge

CB2 1RS

Tel: +44 1223 359750

www.scudamores.com/

Imagine lazy summer days, drifting along in a punt. A visit to Cambridge would not be complete without spending a few hours floating gently along the River Cam. Established in 1903 Scudamore's is the oldest punting company in Cambridge and visitors and residents can be sure of a genuine punting experience.

There are organised tours or you can hire a punt for an hour or a day and float past the sights that inspired writers

CAMBRIDGE TRAVEL GUIDE

and artists alike. Lord Byron and Rupert Brooke were frequent visitors to Cambridge and you can visit the haunts of these literary greats. Float gently along the river drifting past the Bridge of Sighs and the Wren Library

Punts are available to hire 364 days a year, depending on the weather. The fee is £22 per hour or £90 per day. There are discounts for booking online.

🌍 Kettle's Yard

Castle St

Cambridge

CB3 0AQ

Tel: +44 1223 748100

www.kettlesyard.co.uk/

In 1956 Helen and Jim Ede moved to Cambridge and

CAMBRIDGE TRAVEL GUIDE

converted four cottages into a welcoming place to display their collection of 20th century art. Jim Ede had been a curator for the Tate Gallery for many years and had amassed quite a collection. They were quite happy to give visitors a personal tour round and ten years later gave the house and art collection to the University of Cambridge.

This remarkable collection features works by Henry Moore, Joan Miro, Barbara Hepworth, David Jones and Christopher Wood.

Admission is free and the gallery is open Tuesday to Sunday from 11.30m to 5pm and the house from noon to 5pm.

CAMBRIDGE TRAVEL GUIDE

🌍 Scott Polar Research Institute

Lensfield Road

Cambridge

CB2 1EP

Tel: +44 1223 336540

www.spri.cam.ac.uk/

The Scott Polar Research Institute is a national memorial to Captain Robert Falcon Scott and was founded in 1920. A sub-department of the University of Cambridge it is a centre for research into glaciology and the worldwide polar regions.

The Polar Museum is full of artefacts and collections from the Arctic including the last letters from Scott and photos of the Antarctic by Herbert Pointing.

CAMBRIDGE TRAVEL GUIDE

There are permanent exhibits dedicated to Arctic Exploration, Antarctic Exploration and Modern Polar Science and Glaciology. The museum is designed to encourage families and children as well as scientists and students. There are interactive and hands-on displays to encourage visitors to understand more about these amazing regions of our world.

In the Polar Cinema short films tell about the geography of the area and the bravery of those who have tackled these frozen wastelands as well as the art and lives of the local people.

A wide range of gifts are available in the Polar shop. From mugs to multi-media and cards to clothing, some items are for fun and some are for education and information about the Arctic and Antarctic regions.

CAMBRIDGE TRAVEL GUIDE

The Polar Museum is open Tuesday to Saturday from 10am to 4pm. Admission is free but donations are appreciated.

🌍 Sedgwick Museum of Earth Sciences

Downing Street

Cambridge

CB2 3EQ

Tel: +44 1223 333456

www.sedgwickmuseum.org/

This fascinating museum has a collection of around 1.5 million specimens of fossils, minerals and rocks covering a period of some three billion years. Started by Dr. John

CAMBRIDGE TRAVEL GUIDE

Woodward in the 17th century the original cabinets he kept his displays in are still in use today.

The sections of the museums include Local Geology, Planet Earth, Ancient Life, Darwin the Geologist and the Mineral Gallery. A walk through the museum takes visitors on a journey through the evolution of life. Starting with the building blocks of planets to fossilised animals and plants it is a fascinating glimpse into how our world was formed.

In the museum shop minerals and fossils can be purchased as well as model dinosaurs, jewellery, books, toys and souvenirs.

The Sedgewick Museum is open Monday to Friday 10am to 1pm and 2pm to 5pm and admission is free.

CAMBRIDGE TRAVEL GUIDE

🌍 Shepreth Wildlife Park

Station Rd

Shepreth

Cambs.

SG8 6PZ

Tel: +44 1763 262226

www.sheprethwildlifepark.co.uk/

Just a few miles from the historical sights and educational wonders in Cambridge city centre is the wonderful Shepreth Wildlife Park. It is a great place for a family day out away from dusty books and architecture.

The park opened in 1984 as a centre for injured and orphaned animals like swans, foxes, bats, monkeys, owls, and polecats. In the 1990's many exotic pets were being abandoned as their owners found newer and more fascinating hobbies and they also found their way to Shepreth. Now the park is a conservation charity as well as a hedgehog hospital.

There are various events through the day to watch and sometimes take part in; Keeper Talks, Bug Experience, Birds of Prey Display, Nocturnal House Feeding and Tiger Talk and Feeding are just a few. In the shop visitors can purchase birdseed and fish food to feed to the hungry waterfowl and fish in the lake. An adoption scheme allows visitors to adopt their favourite animal and receive regular updates.

There are lots of exciting events held throughout the year and special Experience days that can be booked. Children and adults can become general zoo keepers for

CAMBRIDGE TRAVEL GUIDE

the day or maybe you fancy being a tiger keeper for a couple of hours.

Admission prices are £11 for adults and £9 for concessions. Family discount tickets are available on line.

Shepreth Wildlife Park is open from April to October every day from 10am to 5.30pm and November to March from 10am to 4.30pm. From November 1st to February half-term the park is closed on Tuesdays and Wednesdays.

🌐 Duxford Imperial War Museum

Duxford

Cambridge

CB22 4QR

Tel: +44 1223 835000

CAMBRIDGE TRAVEL GUIDE

www.iwm.org.uk/

A short drive through the Cambridgeshire countryside will bring you to the Duxford Imperial War Museum. It is Britain's largest aviation museum and home to around 200 aircraft as well as military vehicles and small naval vessels. There are also several small museums including the Royal Anglian Regiment and the Parachute Regiment.

There are seven exhibition buildings, some purpose built and others that are the original Battle of Britain hangars. Duxford is still an active airfield and holds regular air shows. During the Second World War Duxford was the home of RAF squadrons and several specialist and tacticians of the Air Fighting Development Unit.

CAMBRIDGE TRAVEL GUIDE

Two highlights of the exhibition are a pre-production Concorde G-AXDN 101 and a de Havilland Comet. A replica Hawker Hurricane guards the entrance gates and there is a Comet tank to be admired as well as a surface-to-air missile and 9.2-inch artillery piece from the Rock of Gibraltar.

It is a super place for a day out and for refreshments visit the restaurant and café or pack a picnic basket and enjoy the wide open green spaces. For children there is an exciting adventure playground and in the school holidays a varied programme of events keeps the children entertained. In the bright and airy gift shop there are pocket money aviation souvenirs as well as items for more serious collectors.

CAMBRIDGE TRAVEL GUIDE

Duxford Imperial War Museum is open daily at 10am and closes at 4pm in the winter and 6pm in the summer. An adult ticket costs £17.50 with concessions paying £14. Children under 16 are admitted free of charge. Different charges may apply on days when there are air shows or flying displays.

Newmarket Races

Rowley Mile Racecourse & July Racecourse

Newmarket

Suffolk

CB8 0TF

Tel: +44 1638 675500

www.newmarketracecourses.co.uk

For a fantastic day, or evening out, drive the 20 or so

CAMBRIDGE TRAVEL GUIDE

miles from Cambridge to the pretty town of Newmarket and spend some time, and money, at the races.

There has been racing at Newmarket since the days of James II and as well as the two racecourses there are the National Horseracing Museum, Tattersalls and the National Stud.

Newmarket in Suffolk is the headquarters of British horseracing with more training yards than anywhere else in the country. Early every morning strings of beautifully turned out racehorses trot through the town on the way to the practice gallops, each rider with dreams of being a champion jockey one day.

Newmarket has two separate racecourses each with their own distinct personality. The spring and autumn meetings

CAMBRIDGE TRAVEL GUIDE

are held on the Rowley Mile Racecourse which is closest to the town. The Millennium Grandstand on the Rowley Mile is one of the leading conference and exhibition centres for East Anglia with wedding fairs, antiques fairs and dogs shows being held there as well as many private and corporate events.

In the summer months of July and August the race meetings are held at the pretty July Racecourse with its garden party atmosphere. Think of frosty jugs of Pimm's decorated with mint and bowls of strawberries and cream. Friday night race meetings through the summer months are not just about horses though. When the last race is over the pulsating sounds of music can be heard across the marquees and stables as the weekly line-up of top class entertainment gets under way.

CAMBRIDGE TRAVEL GUIDE

The racing season at Newmarket begins in April with the Craven Meeting, and ends in October with the Houghton Meeting. On the Rowley Mile Racecourse the Guineas Meeting in May has been running for over 200 years and is one of the biggest meetings on the racing calendar.

In the height of summer the July Festival incorporating Ladies Day offers three days of fantastic racing with the chance to dress to impress. The Best Dressed Lady Competition is always well attended with an assortment of the most elegant, and sometimes outrageous, outfits and hats.

There is a variety of enclosures on both racecourses whether you want to take the family or be a VIP for the day. In the Family Enclosure you can picnic on the beautifully manicured lawns or at the other end of the

CAMBRIDGE TRAVEL GUIDE

scale take a private box for the day. There are superb restaurants with views across the track and finishing post as well as self-service cafeterias, hot dog stands, seafood kiosks, sandwich bars and ice cream stands.

Prices for admission and packages vary widely but the Newmarket Racecourse website has comprehensive details. As an example admission to the Premium Enclosure for Ladies Day would be £40 per adult and for the Family Enclosure £10 per adult. This includes car parking but does not include any food or drinks.

CAMBRIDGE TRAVEL GUIDE

Budget Tips

🌐 Accommodation

Home From Home Guest House

78 Milton Road, Cambridge, CB4 1LA

Tel: +44 1223 323555

www.homefromhomeguesthouse-cambridge.co.uk/

CAMBRIDGE TRAVEL GUIDE

It would be hard to be more centrally located in Cambridge than at this guest house.

It is just minutes away from Magdalene College, Jesus College and Jesus Green. This guest house is great for sightseeing in and around Cambridge with excellent connections to the M11 and A14 roads.

There are five ensuite bedrooms and one double room with a separate bathroom nearby. All the rooms are equipped with LCD television, free Wifi and a hospitality tray. Cots and children's beds can be supplied on request.

Amenities included free parking, laundry facilities and luggage storage. A double room starts at around £85 for two people sharing including breakfast.

CAMBRIDGE TRAVEL GUIDE

Alpha Milton Guest House

61-63 Milton Rd

Cambridge

CB4 1XA

Tel: +44 1223 311625

www.alphamilton.com/

Only a short stroll from St Mary's Church and the Fitzwilliam Museum in the beautiful city of Cambridge is the Alpha Milton guest house. There is a cosy lounge area for relaxing in as well as a spacious garden for those summer evenings.

There are ten well equipped bedrooms in this friendly guest house. All the rooms are ensuite with flat-screen televisions, desks, hospitality tray and free Wifi. There are single, double or family rooms sleeping up to five people to choose from.

Prices are from £40 per person per night for two people sharing. Breakfast is available but is not included in the room rate.

Cambridge Colleges

www.universityrooms.com/

Follow in the footsteps of some of the most famous students to attend these hallowed halls. Prince Charles, Darwin, Wordsworth and John Cleese all studied in this historic city. Guests can eat in the college hall, wander at leisure through the grounds and learn about the history of Cambridge and enjoy a drink in the college bar.

CAMBRIDGE TRAVEL GUIDE

Rooms vary widely from college to college but all the rooms are centrally located and offer clean, comfortable accommodation at a reasonable rate. Bathroom facilities are usually on a shared basis. Breakfast is sometimes included but check with each individual college when booking. Rates start from around £50 per person per night.

Chapel Street B&B

5 Chapel Street

Cambridge, CB41BY

Tel: +44 1223 514856

www.5chapelstreet.com/

Set in a beautiful 18th century Georgian townhouse Chapel Street B&B is within walking distance to museums, parks and gardens in Cambridge city centre.

CAMBRIDGE TRAVEL GUIDE

There is free public car parking close by or if guests arrive by public transport the B&B offers the free use of bicycles for sightseeing.

The ensuite bedrooms are all comfortably furnished with central heating, television, free Wifi and a full English or continental breakfast is included. There are three bedrooms, two doubles and one twin. Prices start at £50 per person per night for two sharing.

Arbury Lodge

82 Arbury Rd

Cambridge

CB4 2JE

Tel: +44 1223 364319

www.arburylodgeguesthouse.co.uk/

CAMBRIDGE TRAVEL GUIDE

With excellent access from the A14/M11 junction and A10 this comfortable guest house is only 1.5 miles from the city centre.

This family run guest house offers bright and comfortable rooms, all non-smoking and ensuite. There is free Wifi throughout the building and a large secure car park for guests to use.

Breakfast is included and there is a pretty garden for guests to relax in. Children are welcome and cots and highchairs can be provided. The price is from £40 per person per night.

CAMBRIDGE TRAVEL GUIDE

🌍 Restaurants, Cafés & Bars

Sticky Beaks Café

42 Hobson St

Cambridge

CB1 1NL

Tel: +44 1223 359397

www.stickybeakscafe.co.uk/

It is hard to find anywhere these days that is still individual and Sticky Beaks fits this bill nicely. Hidden away in the back streets of the city centre it is worth searching out. Bright and light inside with a couple of tables outside for warm days this is a great place to rest weary feet.

There is a breakfast and lunch menu as well as snacks and cakes and they serve vegetarian and gluten-free foods. The cake range is particularly popular with delicious treats such as berry and white chocolate bread pudding and peanut butter cake.

Sticky Fingers is open Monday to Friday 8am to 5.50pm, Saturday 9am to 5.30pm and Sunday 10am to 5pm.

Camyoga Café

Central Studios

Thomas House

14 George IV Street

Cambridge

CB2 1HH

Tel: +44 1223 847930

www.camyoga.co.uk/

Camyoga Café in central Cambridge offers a vast range

CAMBRIDGE TRAVEL GUIDE

of contemporary and healthy vegetarian, vegan and gluten free foods. Food can be eaten in the café or taken away if you are in a hurry. There are superfood snacks for energy; soups, salads, sandwiches and smoothies as well as an excellent range of teas and coffees and homemade cakes.

There is a vegan brunch once a month and special events are held where new foods can be sampled. Camyoga is open Monday to Friday 9am to 9pm and Saturday and Sunday 9am to 6pm.

The Table

85 Regent Street

Cambridge

CB2 1AW

Tel: +44 1223 314230

CAMBRIDGE TRAVEL GUIDE

Great food with craft beer from British micro-breweries and a good wine selection is the best way to describe The Table. The delicious handmade thin-crust pizzas are made with their own recipe sourdough topped with the freshest high-quality ingredients.

This is a super place for groups as the large 16 seater table makes an ideal place to sit. There are plenty of smaller tables and some cosy booths for romantic trysts.

The Table is open Wednesday to Sunday from 11am to 9.30pm and is easy to find. Regent Street is the main road from the train station to the city centre and not far from Parker's Piece.

CAMBRIDGE TRAVEL GUIDE

Clowns Café

54 King Street

Cambridge

CB1 1LN

Tel: +44 1223 355711

Clowns Café has been in Cambridge for years.

It is run by a really friendly Italian family who will make you feel welcome whether you drop in for a quick coffee or a full breakfast.

Everywhere is decorated with clowns; on the walls, on the shelves and hanging from the ceilings. If you suffer from coulrophobia, a fear of clowns, it might not be the best place to visit!

CAMBRIDGE TRAVEL GUIDE

However, if happy painted faces don't scare you off, the food is good and the owner brews his own beer. Lasagna and pasta dishes are served in decent sized portions and the tiramisu makes an excellent dessert.

Clowns is open from 8am to 11pm every day.

Gardenia

2 Rose Crescent

Cambridge

CB2 3LL

Tel: +44 1223 356354

Nicknamed Gardies by the locals this is the place to go for fantastic Greek food. Not a restaurant as such but for anyone that is hungry on the way home after a night out this is definitely the place to visit.

The spicy Greek sausages are incredibly popular as are the falafels and kebabs. For cheeseburger fans the ones Gardenia serves are huge and it can get very messy eating them! It is all basic fast food but all delicious, vegetarians can have amazing chip butties, served in warm pitta bread with dollops of creamy mayonnaise.

Gardenia is open from 11.30am to 11pm seven days a week and sometimes later at weekends. It is popular and long queues can form but it always worth the wait.

🌐 Shopping

Grafton Centre

Cambridge

CB1 1PS

Tel: 01223 316201

www.graftoncentre.co.uk

The Grafton Centre has been a favourite of Cambridge shoppers for many years. With plenty of parking and serviced by the park and ride service as well as local buses getting there is easy. The shopping centre is only a ten minute walk from the city centre across Christ's Piece and there is plenty on offer for everyone.

In the Grafton Centre there is plenty of choice with individual fashion shops with all the familiar brand names

CAMBRIDGE TRAVEL GUIDE

and a Debenhams department store. Chemists, hairdressers, jewellers, shoe shops, sports stores and phone shops all have enticing window displays to try to part you from your cash.

There is a year round entertainment programme ranging from make-up master classes to fashion shows, charity events and much more. Special Kids Fun Packs are available in the centre to keep little ones amused while parents get on with some serious shopping.

The Food Court has a variety of places to choose from whether you want a snack or a full meal. The fast food restaurants, cafés and the Italian Restaurant are open from 10am to 10.30pm so ideal for late-night shoppers or visitors to the eight screen cinema.

CAMBRIDGE TRAVEL GUIDE

The shops in the Grafton Centre are open Monday to Friday 9am to 5.30pm with late night to 8pm on Wednesday. At the weekends the opening hours are Saturday 9am to 6pm and Sunday 11am to 5pm.

Cambridge Markets

Market Square

Cambridge

Tel: +44 1223 457000.

From Monday to Saturday the general market traders set up their stalls in the pretty market square in the city centre.

There has been a market here since the Middle Ages and while the goods on offer might have changed the friendly service remains the same.

CAMBRIDGE TRAVEL GUIDE

There is a vast selection of goods, from home grown fruit and vegetables to bike repairs and a tailoring service. Open 10am to 4pm

On Sundays and Bank Holidays the market square is home to the Arts & Crafts market. All the stall holders on these days make or grow their own products whether it is local cheese, meat, wines, furniture, pottery or jewellery. Open 10am to 4pm.

The stalls are all covered with brightly coloured canopies while attractive bedding plants around the central fountain and seating area make a colourful place to rest awhile.

CAMBRIDGE TRAVEL GUIDE

Mill Road Shopping Mile

Mill Road

Cambridge

www.mill-road.com/

For a diverse and bohemian range of shops and places to eat Mill Road is a great place to wander along. Not just Mill Road but there are many side streets where independent and unusual shops can be found. Recently shortlisted by a national newspaper as one the ten best high streets in the UK, Mill Road has also featured in the BBC's Antiques Roadshow programme.

There is a lot of local history in the Mill Road area and a grant from the Heritage Lottery Fund has brought together local residents and traders to keep the memories going.

CAMBRIDGE TRAVEL GUIDE

Mill Road was home to the local Workhouse, Maternity Hospital and the Isolation Hospital as well as having the first cinema, supermarket and railway in Cambridge.

Shops range from antiques and collectables to tattoo parlours, electrical shops, black and afro beauty specialists and Chinese herbal medicine. There is a betting shop, charity shops, pubs and places to eat and drink. Opening times will vary from shop to shop.

Jacks on Trinity

4 Trinity Street

Cambridge

CB2 1TB

Tel: +44 1223 354403

www.jacksontrinity.co.uk/

CAMBRIDGE TRAVEL GUIDE

For lovers of all things British and those looking for souvenirs to take home this shop has to be top of the list. Union Jacks, Cambridge gifts and British icons are to be found here, jostling for space side by side in this mainly red, white and blue shop.

There are great reminders of a visit to the UK from button badges to elegant bone china mugs and leather bags. A handy reusable tote bag is a great way of carrying all your purchases; with a Union Jack on of course! There are fun items and nostalgia items and a range of clothing to suit all ages.

Jacks on Trinity is open 9.30am to 5.30pm Monday to Saturday and 11am to 5pm on Sunday. Throughout July and August the shop opens at 9am Monday to Saturday and 11am Sunday and closes at 7.30pm every day.

Cambridge Toy Shop

5/16 Sussex Street

Cambridge

CB1 1PA

Tel: +44 1223 309010

www.cambridgetoyshop.co.uk/

Grown-ups and children will love this shop. Spread out over two floors around 9,000 toys and games ranging from the latest hi-tech gadgets to old-fashioned wooden toys can be found here.

There are toys for newborns and young children as well as ride-on toys or try your hand at creative play or arts and crafts. There are outdoor toys for long summer days

CAMBRIDGE TRAVEL GUIDE

and books, puzzles and games for when staying inside is a better idea.

The staff are helpful and knowledgeable about the products and there is a personal shopper service and gifts can be wrapped if required.

The Cambridge Toy Shop is open Monday to Saturday from 9.30am to 5.30pm and Sunday 11am to 5pm.

CAMBRIDGE TRAVEL GUIDE

🌐 Entry Requirements

Citizens of the European Union do not need a visa when visiting the UK. Non-EU members from European countries within the European Economic Area (EEA) are also exempt. This includes countries like Iceland, Norway, Liechtenstein and Switzerland. Visitors from Canada, Australia, Japan, Malaysia, Hong Kong SAR, New Zealand, Singapore, South Korea and the USA do not need a visa to visit the UK, provided that their stay does not exceed 6 months. Visitors from Oman, Qatar and the United Arab Emirates may apply for an Electronic Visa Waiver (EVW) via the internet, if their stay in the UK is less than 6 months. You will need a visa to visit the UK, if travelling from India, Jamaica, Cuba, South Africa, Thailand, the People's Republic of China, Saudi Arabia, Zimbabwe, Indonesia, Cambodia, Nigeria, Ghana, Kenya, Egypt, Ethiopia, Vietnam, Turkey, Taiwan, Pakistan, Russia, the Philippines, Iran, Afghanistan and more. If you are in doubt about the status of your country, do inquire with officials of the relevant UK Embassy, who should be able to advise you. Visitors from the EU (European Union) or EEA (European Economic Area) will not require immigration clearance when staying in the Isle of Man, but may require a work permit if they wish to take employment there. If needed, a visa for the Isle of Man may be obtained from the British Embassy or High Commission in your country. Applications can be made via the Internet.

CAMBRIDGE TRAVEL GUIDE

If you wish to study in the UK, you will need to qualify for a student visa. There are a number of requirements. First, you have to provide proof of acceptance into an academic institution and available funding for tuition, as well as monthly living costs. A health surcharge of £150 will be levied for access to the National Health Service. Applications can be made online and will be subject to a points based evaluation system.

If you need to visit the UK for professional reasons, there are several different classes of temporary work visas. Charity volunteers, sports professionals and creative individuals can qualify for a stay of up to 12 months, on submission of a certificate of sponsorship. Nationals from Canada, Australia, Japan, Monaco, New Zealand, Hong Kong, Taiwan and the Republic of Korea can also apply for the Youth Mobility Scheme that will allow them to work in the UK for up to two years, if they are between the ages of 18 and 30. Citizens of Commonwealth member countries may qualify for an ancestral visa that will enable them to stay for up to 5 years and apply for an extension.

CAMBRIDGE TRAVEL GUIDE

Health Insurance

Visitors from the European Union or EEA (European Economic Area) countries are covered for using the UK's National Health Service, by virtue of a European Health Insurance Card (EHIC). This includes visitors from Switzerland, Liechtenstein, the Canary Islands and Iceland. The card can be applied for free of charge. If you are in doubt about the process, the European Commission has created phone apps for Android, IPhone and Windows to inform European travellers about health matters in various different countries.

Bear in mind that a slightly different agreement is in place for Crown Dependencies, such as the Isle of Man and the Channel Islands. There is a reciprocal agreement between the UK and the Isle of Man with regards to basic healthcare, but this does not include the option of repatriation, which could involve a considerable expense, should facilities such as an Air Ambulance be required. If visiting the UK from the Isle of Man, do check the extent of your health insurance before your departure. A similar reciprocal agreement exists between the UK and the Channel Islands. This covers basic emergency healthcare, but it is recommended that you inquire about travel health insurance if visiting the UK from the Channel Islands.

CAMBRIDGE TRAVEL GUIDE

The UK has a reciprocal healthcare agreement with several countries including Australia, New Zealand, Barbados, Gibraltar, the Channel Islands, Montserrat, Romania, Turkey, Switzerland, the British Virgin Islands, the Caicos Islands, Bulgaria, the Falkland Islands and Anguilla, which means that nationals of these countries are covered when visiting the UK. In some cases, only emergency care is exempted from charges. Reciprocal agreements with Armenia, Azerbaijan, Belarus, Georgia, Kazakhstan, Kyrgyzstan, Moldova, Russia, Tajikistan, Turkmenistan, Ukraine and Uzbekistan were terminated at the beginning of 2016 and no longer apply.

Visitors from non European countries without medical insurance will be charged 150 percent of the usual rate, should they need to make use of the National Health Service (NHS). Exemptions exist for a number of categories, including refugees, asylum seekers. Anyone with a British work permit is also covered for health care. Find out the extent of your health cover before leaving home and make arrangements for adequate travel insurance, if you need additional cover.

Travelling with pets

If travelling from another country within the EU, your pet will be able to enter the UK without quarantine, provided that

CAMBRIDGE TRAVEL GUIDE

certain entry requirements are met. The animal will need to be microchipped and up to date on rabies vaccinations. This means that the vaccinations should have occurred no later than 21 days before your date of departure. In the case of dogs, treatment against tapeworm must also be undertaken before your departure. You will need to carry an EU pet passport. If travelling from outside the EU, a third-country official veterinary certificate will need to be issued within 10 days of your planned departure. Check with your vet or the UK embassy in your country about specific restrictions or requirements for travel with pets.

In the case of cats travelling from Australia, a statement will need to be issued by the Australian Department of Agriculture to confirm that your pet has not been in contact with carriers of the Hendra virus. If travelling from Malaysia, you will need to carry documentation from a vet that your pet has tested negative for the Nipah virus within 10 days before your departure. There are no restrictions on pet rodents, rabbits, birds, reptilians, fish, amphibians or reptiles, provided that they are brought from another EU country. For pet rabbits and rodents from countries outside the European Union, a four month quarantine period will be required, as well as a rabies import licence. Entry is prohibited for prairie dogs from the USA and squirrels and rodents from sub-Saharan Africa.

CAMBRIDGE TRAVEL GUIDE

🌐 Airports, Airlines & Hubs

Airports

London, the capital of England and the UK's most popular tourist destination is served by no less than 6 different airports. Of these, the best known is **Heathrow International Airport (LHR)**, which ranks as the busiest airport in the UK and Europe and sixth busiest in the world. Heathrow is located about 23km to the west of the central part of London. It is utilized by more than 90 airlines and connects to 170 destinations around the world. The second busiest is **Gatwick Airport (LGW)**, which lies 5km north of Crawley and about 47km south of the central part of London. Its single runway is the world's busiest and in particular, it offers connections to the most popular European destinations. From 2013, it offered travellers a free flight connection service, called Gatwick Connect if the service is not available through their individual airlines. **London Luton Airport (LTN)** is located less than 3km from Luton and about 56km north of London's city center. It is the home of EasyJet, the UK's largest airline, but also serves as a base for Monarch, Thomson Airlines and Ryanair. **London Stansted Airport (STN)** is the fourth busiest airport in the UK. Located about 48km northeast of London, it is an important base for Ryanair and also utilized by EasyJet, Thomas Cook Airline and Thomson Airways. **London Southend Airport (SEN)** is

CAMBRIDGE TRAVEL GUIDE

located in Essex, about 68km from London's central business area. Once the third busiest airport in London, it still handles air traffic for EasyJet and Flybe. Although **City Airport (LCY)** is the nearest to the city center of London, its facilities are compact and limiting. The short runway means that it is not really equipped to handle large aircraft and the airport is not operational at night either. It is located in the Docklands area, about 6.4km from Canary Wharf and mainly serves business travellers. Despite these restrictions, it is still the 5th busiest airport in London and 13th busiest in Europe.

The UK's third busiest airport is **Manchester International Airport (MAN)**, which is located about 13.9km southwest of Manchester's CBD. **Birmingham Airport (BHX)** is located 10km from Birmingham's CBD and offers connections to domestic as well as international destinations. **Newcastle International Airport (NCL)** is located about 9.3km from Newcastle's city center and offers connections to Tyne and Wear, Northumberland, Cumbria, North Yorkshire and even Scotland. **Leeds/Bradford Airport (LBA)** provides connections to various cities in the Yorkshire area, including Leeds, Bradford, York and Wakefield. **Liverpool International Airport (LPL)**, also known as Liverpool John Lennon Airport, serves the north-western part of England and provides connections to destinations in Germany, France, Poland, the Netherlands, Spain, Greece, Cyprus, the USA, the Canary

CAMBRIDGE TRAVEL GUIDE

Islands, Malta, Jersey and the Isle of Man. **Bristol Airport (BRS)** provides international access to the city of Bristol, as well as the counties of Somerset and Gloucestershire. As the 9th busiest airport in the UK, it also serves as a base for budget airlines such as EasyJet and Ryanair. **East Midlands Airport (EMA)** connects travellers to Nottingham.

Edinburgh Airport (EDI) is the busiest in Scotland and one of the busier airports in the UK. Its primary connections are to London, Bristol, Birmingham, Belfast, Amsterdam, Paris, Frankfurt, Dublin and Geneva. Facilities include currency exchange, a pet reception center and tourist information desk. **Glasgow International Airport (GLA)** is the second busiest airport in Scotland and one of the 10 busiest airports of the UK. As a gateway to the western part of Scotland, it also serves as a primary airport for trans-Atlantic connections to Scotland and as a base for budget airlines such as Ryanair, Flybe, EasyJet and Thomas Cook. **Cardiff Airport (CWL)** lies about 19km west of the city center of Cardiff and provides access to Cardiff, as well as the south, mid and western parts of Wales. In particular, it offers domestic connections to Glasgow, Edinburgh, Belfast, Aberdeen and Newcastle. **Belfast International Airport (BFS)** is the gateway to Northern Ireland and welcomes approximately 4 million passengers per year. **Kirkwall Airport (KOI)** was originally built for use by the RAF in 1940, but reverted to civilian aviation from 1948. It is located near the town of

CAMBRIDGE TRAVEL GUIDE

Kirkwall and serves as gateway to the Orkney Islands. It is mainly utilized by the regional Flybe service and the Scottish airline, Loganair. The airports at **Guernsey (GCI)** and **Jersey (JER)** offer access to the Channel Islands.

Airlines

British Airways (BA) is the UK's flag carrier airline and was formed around 1972 from the merger of British Overseas Airways Corporation (BOAC) and British European Airways (BEA). It has the largest fleet in the UK and flies to over 160 destinations on 6 different continents. A subsidiary, BA CityFlyer, manages domestic and European connections. British Airways Limited maintains an executive service linking London to New York. The budget airline EasyJet is based at London Luton Airport. In terms of annual passenger statistics, it is Britain's largest airline and Europe's second largest airline after Ryanair. With 19 bases around Europe, it fosters strong connections with Italy, France, Germany and Spain. Thomas Cook Airlines operates as the air travel division of the Thomas Cook group, Britain and the world's oldest travel agent. Thomson Airways is the world's largest charter airline, resulting from a merger between TUI AG and First Choice Holidays. The brand operates scheduled and chartered flights connecting Ireland and the UK with Europe, Africa, Asia and North

CAMBRIDGE TRAVEL GUIDE

America. Founded in the 1960s, Monarch Airlines still operates under the original brand identity and maintains bases at Leeds, Birmingham, Gatwick and Manchester. Its primary base is at London Luton Airport. Jet2.com is a budget airline based at Leeds/Bradford, which offers connections to 57 destinations. Virgin Atlantic, the 7th largest airline in the UK, operates mainly from its bases at Heathrow, Gatwick and Manchester Airport.

Flybe is a regional, domestic service which provides connections to UK destinations. Covering the Channel Islands, Flybe is in partnership with Blue Islands, an airline based on the island of Guernsey. Blue Islands offers connections from Guernsey to Jersey, London, Southampton, Bristol, Dundee, Zurich and Geneva. Loganair is a regional Scottish airline which is headquartered at Glasgow International Airport. It provides connections to various destinations in Scotland, including Aberdeen, Edinburgh, Inverness, Norwich and Dundee. Additionally it operates a service to the Shetland Islands, the Orkney Islands and the Western Islands in partnership with Flybe. BMI Regional, also known as British Midland Regional Limited, is based at East Midlands Airport and offers connections to other British destinations such as Aberdeen, Bristol and Newcastle, as well as several cities in Europe.

CAMBRIDGE TRAVEL GUIDE

Hubs

Heathrow Airport serves as a primary hub for British Airways. Gatwick Airport serves as a hub for British Airways and EasyJet. EasyJet is based at London Luton Airport, but also maintains a strong presence at London's Stansted Airport and Bristol Airport. Manchester Airport serves as a hub for the regional budget airline Flybe, as does Birmingham Airport. Thompson Airways maintain bases at three of London's airports, namely Gatwick, London Luton and Stansted, as well as Belfast, Birmingham, Bournemouth, Bristol, Cardiff, Doncaster/Sheffield, East Midlands, Edinburgh, Exeter, Glasgow, Leeds/Bradford, Manchester and Newcastle. Jet2.com has bases at Leeds/Bradford, Belfast, East Midlands, Edinburgh, Glasgow, Manchester and Newcastle. Glasgow International Airport serves as the primary hub for the Scottish airline, Loganair, which also has hubs at Edinburgh, Dundee, Aberdeen and Inverness.

Sea Ports

As the nearest English port to the French coast, Dover in Kent has been used to facilitate Channel crossings to the European mainland for centuries. This makes it one of the busiest passenger ports in the world. Annually, 16 million passengers,

CAMBRIDGE TRAVEL GUIDE

2.8 million private vehicles and 2.1 million trucks pass through its terminals. Three ferry services to France are based on the Eastern dock, connecting passengers to ports in Calais and Dunkirk. Additionally, the Port of Dover also has a cruise terminal, as well as a marina.

The Port of Southampton is a famous port on the central part of the south coast of the UK. It enjoys a sheltered location thanks to the proximity of the Isle of Wight and a tidal quirk that favours its facilities for bulky freighters as well as large cruise liners. The port serves as a base for several UK cruise operators including Cunard, Celebrity Cruises, P&O Cruises, Princess Cruises and Royal Caribbean. Other tour operators using its terminals include MSC Cruises, Costa Cruises, Crystal Cruises and Fred. Olsen Cruise Lines. Southampton is a popular departure point for various cruises to European cities such as Hamburg, Rotterdam, Amsterdam, Le Havre, Bruges, Barcelona, Lisbon, Genoa and Scandinavia, as well as trans-Atlantic destinations such as Boston, New York and Miami. A short but popular excursion is the two day cruise to Guernsey. Southampton also offers ferry connections to the Isle of Wight and the village of Hythe. The port has four cruise terminals and is well-connected by rail to London and other locations in the UK.

CAMBRIDGE TRAVEL GUIDE

Eurochannel

The Eurotunnel (or the Channel Tunnel) was completed in 1994 and connects Folkestone in Kent with Coquelles near Calais. This offers travellers a new option for entering the UK from the European continent. Via the Eurostar rail network, passengers travelling to or from the UK are connected with destinations across Europe, including Paris, Brussels, Frankfurt, Amsterdam and Geneva. On the UK side, it connects to the London St Pancras station. Also known as St Pancras International, this station is one of the UK's primary terminals for the Eurostar service. The Eurotunnel Shuttle conveys private and commercial vehicles through the tunnel and provides easy motorway access on either side.

Money Matters

Currency

The currency of the UK is the Pound Sterling. Notes are issued in denominations of £5, £10, £20 and £50. Coins are issued in denominations of £2, £1, 50p, 20p, 10p, 5p, 2p and 1p. Regional variants of the pound are issued in Scotland and Northern Ireland, but these are acceptable as legal tender in other parts of the UK as well. The Isles of Jersey, Guernsey and

CAMBRIDGE TRAVEL GUIDE

Man issue their own currency, known respectively as the Jersey Pound, the Guernsey Pound and the Manx Pound. However, the Pound Sterling (and its Scottish and Northern Irish variants) can also be used for payment on the Isle of Man, Jersey and Guernsey.

Banking/ATMs

ATM machines, also known locally as cashpoints or a hole in the wall, are well distributed in cities and larger towns across the UK. Most of these should be compatible with your own banking network, and may even be enabled to give instructions in multiple languages. A small fee is charged per transaction. Beware of helpful strangers, tampering and other scams at ATM machines. Banking hours vary according to bank group and location, but you can generally expect trading hours between 9.30am and 4.30pm.

Credit Cards

Credit cards are widely accepted at many businesses in the UK, but you may run into smaller shops, restaurants and pubs that do not offer credit card facilities. Cash is still king in the British pub, although most have adapted to credit card use. For hotel bookings or car rentals, credit cards are essential. Visa and MasterCard are most commonly used. Acceptance of American Express and Diners Club is less widespread. Chip and PIN cards are the norm in the UK. While shops will generally have card facilities that can still accept older magnetic strip or US chip-and-signature cards, you will find that ticket machines and self service vendors are not configured for those types of credit cards.

Tourist Tax

A tourist tax of £1 for London has been under discussion, but to date nothing has been implemented. The areas of Cornwall, Brighton, Edinburgh, Westminster and Birmingham also considered implementing a tourist tax, but eventually rejected the idea.

Claiming back VAT

If you are not from the European Union, you can claim back VAT (or Value Added Tax) paid on your purchases in the UK. The VAT rate in the UK is 20 percent, but to qualify for a refund, certain conditions will have to be met. Firstly, VAT can only be claimed merchants participating in a VAT refund program scheme. If this is indicated, you can ask the retailer for a VAT 407 form. You may need to provide proof of eligibility by producing your passport. Customs authorities at your point of departure from the European Union (this could be the UK or another country) will inspect the completed form as well as your purchased goods. You should receive your refund from a refund booth at the airport or from the refund department of the retailer where you bought the goods.

Tipping Policy

It is customary to tip for taxis, restaurants and in bars where you are served by waiting staff, rather than bartenders. The usual rate is between 10 and 15 percent. Some restaurants will add this automatically to your bill as a service charge, usually at a rate of 12.5 percent. Tipping is not expected in most pubs, although you may offer a small sum (traditionally the price of a half pint), with the words "and have one yourself". Some hotels will also add a service charge of between 10 and 15 percent to your bill. You may leave a tip for room-cleaning staff upon departure. Tip bellboys and porters to express your gratitude for a particular service, such as helping with your luggage or organizing a taxi or booking a tour. Tipping is not expected at fast food, self service or takeaway outlets, but if the food is delivered, do tip the delivery person. You may also tip a tour

CAMBRIDGE TRAVEL GUIDE

guide between £2 and £5 per person, or £1 to £2 if part of a family group, especially if the person was attentive, engaging and knowledgeable. In Scotland, most restaurants do not levy a service charge and it is customary to tip between 10 and 15 percent. Tipping in Scottish pubs is not necessary, unless you were served a meal.

Connectivity

Mobile Phones

Like most EU countries, the UK uses the GSM mobile service. This means that visitors from the EU should have no problem using their mobile phones, when visiting the UK. If visiting from the USA, Canada, Japan, India, Brazil or South Korea, you should check with your service provider about compatibility and roaming fees. The US service providers Sprint, Verizon and U.S. Cellular employ the CDMA network, which is not compatible with the UK's phone networks. Even if your phone does use the GSM service, you will still incur extra costs, if using your phone in the UK. For European visitors the rates will vary from 28p per minute for voice calls and 58p per megabyte for data. The alternative option would be to purchase a UK sim card to use during your stay in the UK. It is relatively easy to get a SIM card, though. No proof of identification or

CAMBRIDGE TRAVEL GUIDE

address details will be required and the SIM card itself is often free, when combined with a top-up package.

The UK has four mobile networks. They are Vodafone, O2, Three (3) and EE (Everything Everywhere), the latter of which grew from a merger between Orange and T-Mobile. All of these do offer pay-as-you-go packages that are tailor made for visitors. Through EE, you will enjoy access to a fast and efficient 4G network, as well as 3G and 2G coverage. There is a whole range of pay as you go products, which are still part of the Orange brand. These have been named after different animals, each with a different set of rewards. The dolphin package, which includes free internet and free texts will seem ideal to most tech savvy travellers. The canary plan offers free calls, texts and photo messages, while the raccoon offers the lowest call rate. Also through EE, you can choose from three different package deals, starting from as little as £1 and choose whether to favour data or call time.

With the Three packages, you will get a free SIM with the All-in-One package of £10. Your rewards will include a mix of 500Mb data, 3000 texts and 100 minutes calltime. It is valid for 30 days. Through the O2 network, you can get a free SIM card, when you choose from a selection of different top-up packages, priced from £10. As a service provider, O2 also offers users an international SIM card, which will enable you to call and text

CAMBRIDGE TRAVEL GUIDE

landline as well as mobile numbers in over 200 countries. With Vodafone, you can choose between a mixed top-up package that adds the reward of data to the benefit of voice calls and data only SIM card offer. The packages start at £10.

Alternately, you could also explore the various offers from a range of virtual suppliers, which include Virgin Mobile, Lebara Mobile, Lycamobile, Post Office Mobile and Vectone Mobile. Virtual Packages are also available through the retailers Tesco and ASDA.

Dialling Code

The international dialling code for the UK is +44.

Emergency Numbers

General Emergency: 999
(The European Union General emergency number of 112 can also be accessed in the UK. Calls will be answered by 999 operators)
National Health Service (NHS): 111
Police (non-emergency): 101

CAMBRIDGE TRAVEL GUIDE

MasterCard: 0800 056 0572

Visa: 0800 015 0401

🌐 General Information

Public Holidays

1 January: New Year's Day (if New Year's Day falls on a Saturday or Sunday, the 2nd or 3rd of January may also be declared a public holiday).
17 March: St Patrick's Day (Northern Ireland only)
March/April: Good Friday
March/April: Easter Monday
First Monday in May: May Day Bank Holiday
Last Monday in May: Spring Bank Holiday
12 July: Battle of the Boyne/Orangemen's Day (North Ireland only)
First Monday of August: Summer Bank Holiday (Scotland only)
Last Monday of August: Summer Bank Holiday (everywhere in the UK, except Scotland)
30 November: St Andrew's Day (Scotland only)
25 December: Christmas Day
26 December: Boxing Day

(if Christmas Day or Boxing Day falls on a Saturday or Sunday, 27 and/or 28 December may also be declared a public holiday)

Time Zone

The UK falls in the Western European Time Zone. This can be calculated as Greenwich Mean Time/Co-ordinated Universal Time (GMT/UTC) 0 in winter and +1 in summer for British Summer Time.

Daylight Savings Time

Clocks are set forward one hour at 01.00am on the last Sunday of March and set back one hour at 02.00am on the last Sunday of October for Daylight Savings Time.

School Holidays

In the UK, school holidays are determined by city or regional authorities. This means that it could vary from town to town, but general guidelines are followed. There are short breaks to coincide with Christmas and Easter, as well as short mid terms for winter (in February), summer (around June) and autumn (in

CAMBRIDGE TRAVEL GUIDE

October). A longer summer holiday at the end of the academic year lasts from mid July to the end of August.

Trading Hours

For large shops, trading hours will depend on location. There are outlets for large supermarket chains such as Asda and Tesco that are open round the clock on weekdays or may trade from 6am to 11pm. In England and Wales, the regulations on Sunday trading are set according the size of the shop. While there are no restrictions on shops less than 280 square meters, shops above that size are restricted to 6 hours trading on Sundays and no trading on Christmas or Easter Sunday. Post office trading hours vary according to region and branch. Most post offices are open 7 days a week, but hours may differ according to location.

In Scotland, the trading hours for most shops are from 9am to 5pm, Monday to Saturdays. In larger towns, urban city areas and villages frequented by tourists, many shops will elect to trade on Sundays as well. Some rural shops will however close at 1am on a weekday, which would usually be Wednesday or Thursday. Some shops have introduced late trading hours on Thursdays and longer trading hours may also apply in the summer months and in the run-up to Christmas. On the Scottish islands of Lewis, Harris and North Uist, all shops will be closed on a Sunday.

Driving Policy

In the UK, driving is on the left side of the road. Both front and rear passengers must wear seat belts. If travelling with children, they must be accommodated with an age-appropriate child seat. With rental cars, it is advisable to make prior arrangements for this when you arrange your booking. If stopped by the police, you may be asked for your driver's licence, insurance certificate and MOT certificate, which must be rendered within 7 days. Driving without insurance could result in the confiscation of your vehicle.

In urban and residential areas, the speed limit for all types of vehicles is 48km per hour. On motorways and dual carriageways, cars, motorcycles and motor homes less than 3.05 tonnes are allowed to drive up to 112km per hour. On a single carriageway, this drops to 96km per hour. For motorhomes above 3.05 tonnes and vehicles towing caravans or trailers, the speed limit is 80km for single carriageways and 96km for dual carriageways and motorways. Local speed limits may vary. The alcohol limit for drivers is 35mg per 100ml of breath in England

and Wales and 22mg per 100ml of breath in Scotland (or 80mg and 50mg respectively per 100ml of blood).

Drinking Policy

The legal age for buying alcohol in the UK is 18. Young persons of 16 to 17 may drink a single beer, cider or glass of wine in a pub, provided they are in the company of an adult. From the age of 14, persons can enter a pub unaccompanied to enjoy a meal and children are allowed in pubs with their parents until 9pm. For buying alcohol at an off-license, you will need to be over 21 and may be asked to provide identification.

Smoking Policy

In the UK, smoking is prohibited in public buildings, all enclosed spaces and on public transport. Smoking is also prohibited at bus shelters. The law also states that 'no smoking' signage must be displayed clearly within all premises covered by the legislation. The only exceptions are rooms specifically designated as smoking rooms.

CAMBRIDGE TRAVEL GUIDE

Electricity

Electricity: 230 volts

Frequency: 50 Hz

The UK's electricity sockets are compatible with the Type G plugs, a plug that features three rectangular pins or prongs, arranged in a triangular shape. They are incompatible with the two pronged Type C plugs commonly used on the European continent, as UK sockets are shuttered and will not open without the insertion of the third "earth" pin. If travelling from the USA, you will need a power converter or transformer to convert the voltage from 230 to 110, to avoid damage to your appliances. The latest models of certain types of camcorders, cell phones and digital cameras are dual-voltage, which means that they were manufactured with a built in converter, but you will have to check with your dealer about that.

Food & Drink

England gave the world one of its favourite breakfast, the Full English, a hearty feast of bacon eggs, sausage, fried mushroom and grilled tomato. In the UK, this signature dish is incomplete without a helping of baked beans. In Scotland, you can expect to see black pudding or Lorne sausage added to the ensemble, while the Welsh often throw in some cockles or Laverbread.

CAMBRIDGE TRAVEL GUIDE

For simple, basic meals, you cannot go wrong with traditional pub fare. All round favourites include the beef pie, shepherd's pie, bangers and mash and toasted sandwiches. Fish and chips, served in a rolled up sheet of newsprint, is another firm favourite. For Sunday roast, expect an elaborate spread of roasted meat, roasted potatoes, vegetables and Yorkshire pudding. The national dish of Scotland is, of course, Haggis - sheep's offal which is seasoned and boiled in a sheep's stomach. This dish rises to prominence on Burns Night (25 January), when the birthday of the poet Robert Burns is celebrated. Burns wrote 'Address to a Haggis'. The influence of immigrants to the UK has led to kosher haggis (which is 100 percent free of pork products) and an Indian variant, Haggis pakora, said to have originated from the Sikh community. The synergy of Anglo-Indian cuisine also gave rise to popular dishes such as Chicken Tikka Masala and Kedgeree.

The neighbourhood pub is an integral part of social life in the UK and Britain is known for its dark ale, also referred to as bitter. Currently, the most popular beer in the UK is Carling, a Canadian import which has available in the British Isles since the 1980s. Foster's Lager, the second most popular beer in the UK, is brewed by Scottish & Newcastle, the largest brewery in Britain. For a highly rated local brew, raise a mug of award-winning Fuller's beer. The brewery was established early in the 1800s and produces London Pride, London Porter and Chiswick

CAMBRIDGE TRAVEL GUIDE

Bitter, to name just a few. A popular brand from neighbouring Ireland is Guinness. Along with Indian curries, the market share of Indian beer brands like Jaipur or Cobra beer has grown in recent years. Kent has developed as an emergent wine producer.

On the non-alcoholic side, you can hardly beat tea for popularity. The English like to brew it strong and serve it in a warmed china teapot with generous amounts of milk. Tea is served at 11am and 4pm. Afternoon tea is often accompanied with light snacks, such as freshly baked scones or cucumber sandwiches. High tea, served a little later at 6pm, can be regarded as a meal. A mixture of sweet and savoury treats such as cakes, scones, crumpets, cheese or poached egg on toast, cold meats and pickles. The custom of High Tea goes back to the days when dinner was the midday meal. These days, it is often replaced by supper.

Scotland is known for producing some of the world's finest whiskies. Its industry goes back at least 500 years. One of Scotland's best selling single malt whisky is produced by the famous Glenmorangie distillery in the Highlands. Chivas Brothers, who once supplied whisky by royal warrant to Queen Victoria's Scottish household, produce Chivas Regal, one of the best known blended whiskies of Scotland. The Famous Grouse, which is based at Glenturret near the Highlands town of Crieff, produces several excellent examples of blended grain whiskies.

CAMBRIDGE TRAVEL GUIDE

Bell's Whisky is one of the top selling whiskies in the UK and Europe. Other well known Scottish whisky brands include Old Pulteney, Glen Elgin, Tamdhu (a Speyside distillery that produces single malt), Balvenie, Bunnahabhain, Macallan, Aberlour, Bowmore, the award-winning Ballantine and Grant's whisky, from a distillery that has been run by the same family for five generations. Another proudly Scottish drink is Drambuie, the first liqueur stocked by the House of Lords. According to legend, its recipe was originally gifted to the MacKinnon clan by Bonnie Prince Charlie.

Events

Sports

Horse racing is often called the sport of kings and has enjoyed the support of the British aristocracy for centuries. Here you can expect to rub shoulders with high society and several races go back to the 1700s. The Cheltenham Festival is usually on or near St Patrick's Day and now comprises a four day event of 27 races. The Grand National takes place in Liverpool in April. With prize money of £1 million, this challenging event is Europe's richest steeplechase. A Scottish equivalent of the Grand National takes place in Ayr in the same month. There is

CAMBRIDGE TRAVEL GUIDE

also a Welsh Grand National, which now takes place in the winter at Chepstow. A past winner of Welsh event was none other than the author Dick Francis. Other important horse races are the Guineas at Newmarket (April/May), the Epsom Oaks and the Epsom Derby (first Saturday of June) and the St Leger Stakes, which takes place in Doncaster in September. One of the annual highlights is Royal Ascot week, traditionally attended by the British Royal Family. This takes place in June at Berkshire. There is a strict dress code and access to the Royal Enclosure is limited, especially for first timers. Fortunately, you will be able to view the the arrival of the monarch in a horse drawn carriage with a full royal procession at the start of the day. Another high profile equestrian event is the St Regis International Polo Cup, which takes place in May at Cowdray Park.

Wimbledon, one of the world's top tennis tournaments, takes place in London from last week of June, through to the first half of July. If you are a golfing enthusiast, do not miss the British Open, scheduled for July at Royal Troon in South Ayrshire, Scotland. The event, which has been played since 1860, is the world's oldest golf tournament. A highlight in motorcycle racing is the Manx Grand Prix, which usually takes place in August or September and serves as a great testing ground for future talent. The British Grand Prix takes place at Silverstone in Northamptonshire. A sporting event that occupies a special

CAMBRIDGE TRAVEL GUIDE

place in popular culture is the annual boat race that usually takes place in April between the university teams of Oxford and Cambridge. The tradition goes back to 1829 and draws large numbers of spectators to watch from the banks of the Thames. The FA Cup final, which is played at Wembley Stadium in May, is a must for soccer fans. As a sports event, the London Marathon is over 100 years old and draws entries from around the world to claim its prize money of a million pounds. Keen athletes will only have a brief window period of less than a week to submit their entries. Selection is by random ballot. The 42km race takes place in April.

Cultural

If you want to brush shoulders with some of your favourite authors or get the chance to pitch to a British publisher or agent, you dare not miss the London Book Fair. The event takes place in April and includes talks, panel discussions and exhibitions by a large and diverse selection of publishing role players. The London Art Fair happens in January and features discussions, tours and performances. For comic geeks there are several annual events in the UK to look forward to. The CAPTION comic convention in Oxford, which goes back to the early 1990s, is a must if you want to show your support to Britain's

CAMBRIDGE TRAVEL GUIDE

small presses. There is a Scottish Comic Con that takes place in the Edinburgh International Conference Center in April and a Welsh Comic Con, also in April, at Wrexham. The MCM London Comic Con happens over the last weekends of May and October, and covers anime, manga, cosplay, gaming and science fiction in general. The UK's calendar of film festivals clearly shows its cultural diversity. The oldest events are the London Film Festival (October) and the Leeds Film Festival (November). There are also large events in Manchester and Cambridge. The high-profile Encounters festival for shorts and animated films takes place each September in Bristol.

History fans can immerse themselves in the thrills and delights of the Glastonbury Medieval Fayre, which takes place in April and includes stalls, jousting and minstrels. The Tewkesbury Medieval Festival takes place in summer and its key event is the re-enactment of the Battle of Tewkesbury.

Edinburgh has an annual International Film Festival that takes place in June. The city also hosts a broader cultural festival that takes place in August. The Edinburgh International Festival is a three week event that features a packed programme of music, theatre, dance and opera, as well as talks and workshops. The Royal Highland show takes place in June and features agricultural events as well as show jumping. If you want to experience the massing of Scottish pipers, one good opportunity

CAMBRIDGE TRAVEL GUIDE

is the Braemar Gathering, an event that takes place on the first Saturday in September and is usually attended by the Royal family. Its roots go back 900 years. Over the spring and summer seasons, you can attend numerous Highland Games, which feature Scottish piping, as well as traditional sports such as hammer throw and tug of war. For Scottish folk dancing, attend the Cowal Highland Gathering, which takes place towards the end of August.

Websites of Interest

http://www.visitbritain.com
http://www.myguidebritain.com/
http://wikitravel.org/en/United_Kingdom
http://www.english-heritage.org.uk/
http://www.celticcastles.com/
http://www.tourist-information-uk.com/

Travel Apps

If you are planning to use public transport around the UK, get Journey Pro to help make the best connections.
https://itunes.apple.com/gb/app/journey-pro-london-uk-by-navitime/id388628933

CAMBRIDGE TRAVEL GUIDE

The Around Me app will help you to orient, if you are looking for the nearest ATM, gas station or other convenience services.
http://www.aroundmeapp.com/

If you are worried about missing out on a must-see attraction in a particular area, use the National Trust's app to check out the UK's natural and historical treasures.
http://www.nationaltrust.org.uk/features/app-privacy-policy

Printed in Great Britain
by Amazon